SUGAR GLIDER

By Rachel Rose

Consultant: Andrew Baker, Associate Professor

Minneapolis, Minnesota

Credits
Cover and title page, © Sevendeman/Adobe Stock; 3, © Travis/Adobe Stock and © Adam88xx/Adobe Stock; 4–5, © Anom Harya/Adobe Stock; 6, © DikkyOesin/iStock; 7, © DS light photography/Adobe Stock; 9, © neel/Adobe Stock and © Travis/Adobe Stock; 10–11, © RooM the Agency/Alamy Stock Photo; 11, © LanaLanglois/iStock and © aPhoenix photographer/Shutterstock; 12, © Moonstone Images/Getty Images; 13, © I Wayan Sumatika/Shutterstock; 14, © 4FR/iStock; 14–15, © KAMONRAT/Shutterstock; 17, © Roland Seitre/Minden Pictures; 19, © ANT Photo Library/Science Source; 21, © I Wayan Sumatika/Adobe Stock; 22, © Aleksandar/Adobe Stock; 23, © DSlight_photography/Shutterstock.

Bearport Publishing Company Product Development Team
Publisher: Jen Jenson; Director of Product Development: Spencer Brinker; Managing Editor: Allison Juda; Editor: Cole Nelson; Associate Editor: Naomi Reich; Associate Editor: Tiana Tran; Designer: Kim Jones; Designer: Kayla Eggert; Designer: Steve Scheluchin; Production Specialist: Owen Hamlin

Statement on Usage of Generative Artificial Intelligence
Bearport Publishing remains committed to publishing high-quality nonfiction books. Therefore, we restrict the use of generative AI to ensure accuracy of all text and visual components pertaining to a book's subject. See BearportPublishing.com for details.

Library of Congress Cataloging-in-Publication Data

Names: Rose, Rachel, 1968- author.
Title: Sugar glider / by Rachel Rose.
Description: Minneapolis, Minnesota : Bearport Publishing Company, [2026] | Series: Library of awesome animals | Includes bibliographical references and index.
Identifiers: LCCN 2024057709 (print) | LCCN 2024057710 (ebook) | ISBN 9798895770481 (library binding) | ISBN 9798895774724 (paperback) | ISBN 9798895771655 (ebook)
Subjects: LCSH: Sugar glider--Juvenile literature. | Marsupials--Juvenile literature.
Classification: LCC SF459.S83 R67 2026 (print) | LCC SF459.S83 (ebook) | DDC 636.92--dc23/eng/20250110
LC record available at https://lccn.loc.gov/2024057709
LC ebook record available at https://lccn.loc.gov/2024057710

Copyright © 2026 Bearport Publishing Company. All rights reserved. No part of this publication may be reproduced in whole or in part, stored in any retrieval system, or transmitted in any form or by any means, electronic, mechanical, photocopying, recording, or otherwise, without written permission from the publisher. Bearport Publishing is a division of FlutterBee Education Group.

For more information, write to Bearport Publishing, 5357 Penn Avenue South, Minneapolis, MN 55419.

Contents

Awesome Sugar Gliders!........ 4
Cute Furballs 6
Life Down Under........ 8
Tiny Feet 10
Sweet Treats........12
Survival Skills........ 14
Together in the Trees 16
Baby Boom........ 18
Growing Up 20

Information Station 22
Glossary 23
Index 24
Read More 24
Learn More Online 24
About the Author........ 24

AWESOME Sugar Gliders!

WHOOSH! A sugar glider stretches out its arms and legs, revealing a flap of skin on either side of its body. Then, the **marsupial** jumps, gliding between the trees. Tiny and graceful, sugar gliders are awesome!

SUGAR GLIDERS CAN SOAR MORE THAN 150 FEET (46 M) AT A TIME.

5

Cute Furballs

Sugar gliders are furry creatures with big, round eyes. They are mostly gray-brown with white bellies. Many also have black stripes running down their backs and black markings around their faces. These fuzzy cuties are small. Sugar gliders weigh only 3.3 ounces (110 g). That's lighter than a stick of butter!

WHEN CURLED UP, A SUGAR GLIDER IS OFTEN SMALL ENOUGH TO FIT IN THE PALM OF A PERSON'S HAND.

Life Down Under

Sugar gliders are small **possums** found in forests of eastern Australia. The furry critters are **adapted** to life among the trees. They have a special flap of skin that stretches from their wrists to their ankles, allowing them to glide around their woodsy homes. *WHEE!*

A SUGAR GLIDER'S LONG, BUSHY TAIL HELPS IT BALANCE WHILE GLIDING FROM TREE TO TREE.

Tiny Feet

Sugar gliders are great at grabbing hold of things. Their feet are just as **flexible** as their hands! Opposable fingers and toes on each hand and foot allow the little critters to get a firm grip while climbing. When landing, they use their sharp claws to grab a tight hold. They also use their long claws as combs, brushing themselves clean.

OPPOSABLE FINGERS AND TOES ALSO ALLOW SUGAR GLIDERS TO HOLD ONTO FOOD.

Sweet Treats

How did sugar gliders get their name? It came from their love of sweet foods! Sugar gliders drink the sugary sap from eucalyptus (*yoo*-kuh-LIP-tuhs) and acacia (uh-KAY-shuh) trees in their forest homes. **YUM!** Sugar gliders also dine on the **nectar** and pollen of flowers, as well as on any fruit they can find. These cuties may also eat insects, spiders, or small birds.

SUGAR GLIDERS USE THEIR TEETH TO MAKE HOLES IN TREE BARK TO REACH SAP.

Survival Skills

Because of their small size, sugar gliders are hunted by many **predators**. They need to watch out for owls, domestic cats, and snakes. The marsupials usually use their gliding skills to escape. When scared, sugar gliders may also stand on their back legs with their mouths wide open to make themselves seem bigger.

An owl

Together in the Trees

Sugar gliders stick together in groups called **colonies**. They make their homes high up in the hollows of trees. The animals use their tails to carry leaves and twigs to the perfect spot. Then, they pile them up to make a cozy nest to share.

> SUGAR GLIDERS SLEEP ALL DAY. THEY COME OUT ONLY AT NIGHT.

17

Baby Boom

Sugar gliders usually **mate** several times a year. **Males** seek out many different **female** partners. After about 15 to 17 days, the female sugar gliders give birth to babies called joeys. When these little gliders are born, they are not fully developed. They have no fur and cannot see.

SUGAR GLIDERS MATE IN THE EARLY SPRING.

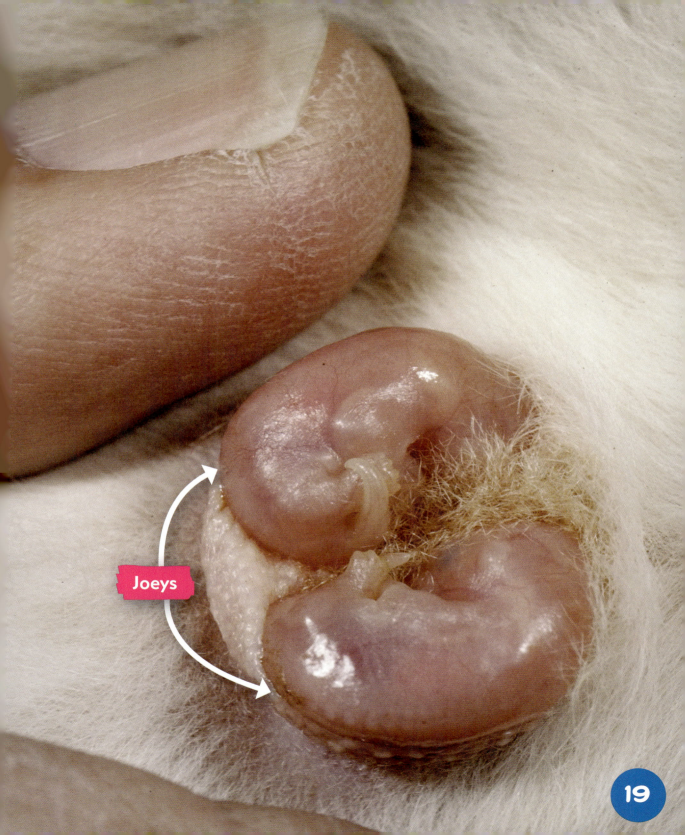

Growing Up

The newly born joeys crawl into their mother's **pouch** where they will finish growing. There, they drink milk from her body and get bigger. After around 10 weeks, the babies are ready to leave the pouch and taste the sweet foods of the forest. When they are 10 months old, the young gliders strike out to start or join new colonies.

WHEN EXPLORING THE WILD, A YOUNG GLIDER MAY CLING TO ITS PARENT'S BACK.

Information Station

SUGAR GLIDERS ARE AWESOME!
LET'S LEARN MORE ABOUT THEM.

Kind of animal: Sugar gliders are mammals. Most mammals have fur, give birth to live young, and drink milk from their mothers as babies.

Other marsupials: There are more than 330 kinds of marsupials, including sugar gliders. Kangaroos, koalas, and quokkas are some other marsupials.

Size: A sugar glider's body can grow up to 8 inches (21 cm) long. That's smaller than a clipboard! But the animal's tail is usually just as long as its body.

SUGAR GLIDERS AROUND THE WORLD

■ Where Sugar Gliders Live

Glossary

adapted changed over time to best fit in an environment

colonies groups of sugar gliders that live together

female a sugar glider that can give birth to young

flexible able to bend easily

males sugar gliders that cannot give birth to young

marsupial a group of mammals that carry babies in pouches on their bodies

mate to come together in order to have young

nectar a sweet liquid found in flowers

possums small marsupials that live in trees

pouch a pocket in a female marsupial's belly used to carry her young

predators animals that hunt and kill other animals for food

Index

acacia 12
Australia 8, 22
eucalyptus 12
females 18
forests 8, 12
Indonesia 8
joeys 18–20
males 18
marsupials 4, 6, 14, 16, 20, 22
mate 18
New Guinea 8
pouch 20
predators 14

Read More

Marie, Renata. *Koalas (Wild About Animals).* Minneapolis: Kaleidoscope, 2022.

McCarthy, Cecilia Pinto. *Rain Forest Biomes (Explore Biomes).* Minneapolis: Abdo Publishing, 2024.

Learn More Online

1. Go to **FactSurfer.com** or scan the QR code below.
2. Enter "**Sugar Glider**" into the search box.
3. Click on the cover of this book to see a list of websites.

About the Author

Rachel Rose writes books for kids and teaches yoga. Her favorite animal of all is her dog, Sandy.